Francis Frith's
Warwick

GRAHAM SUTHERLAND is a retired police inspector who has spent over half his life in Warwick. He has been the Beadle and Town Crier for Warwick for a considerable number of years, and also he is the Ale Taster for Warwick Court Leet. Both he and his wife are Registered Blue Badge Guides for the Heart of England Tourist Board, and they conduct guided walks around Warwick and many other places. Graham gives talks on a variety of subjects, and has written other books on Warwickshire.

Photographic Memories

Francis Frith's
Warwick

_____

Graham Sutherland

FRITH
BOOK Co

First published in the United Kingdom in 2002 by
Frith Book Company Ltd

Paperback Edition 2002
ISBN 1-85937-518-9

Hardback Edition 2002
ISBN 1-85937-678-9

British Library Cataloguing in Publication Data

Francis Frith's Warwick
Graham Sutherland

Frith Book Company Ltd
Frith's Barn, Teffont,
Salisbury, Wiltshire SP3 5QP
Tel: +44 (0) 1722 716 376
Email: info@francisfrith.co.uk
www.francisfrith.co.uk

Printed and bound in Great Britain

Front Cover: Warwick, High Street 1922 72343

Contents

Francis Frith: Victorian Pioneer   7

Frith's Archive - A Unique Legacy   10

Warwick - An Introduction   12

The Approaches into Warwick   14

The River Avon and Mill Street   22

St John's and Smith Street   28

The Town Centre   31

St Mary's Church   42

The Lord Leycester Hospital   44

Warwick Castle   52

Round and About Warwick   58

Index   87

Free Mounted Print Voucher   91

Francis Frith: *Victorian Pioneer*

FRANCIS FRITH, Victorian founder of the world-famous photographic archive, was a complex and multi-talented man. A devout Quaker and a highly successful Victorian businessman, he was both philosophic by nature and pioneering in outlook.

By 1855 Francis Frith had already established a wholesale grocery business in Liverpool, and sold it for the astonishing sum of £200,000, which is the equivalent today of over £15,000,000. Now a multi-millionaire, he was able to indulge his passion for travel. As a child he had pored over travel books written by early explorers, and his fancy and imagination had been stirred by family holidays to the sublime mountain regions of Wales and Scotland. 'What a land of spirit-stirring and enriching scenes and places!' he had written. He was to return to these scenes of grandeur in later years to 'recapture the thousands of vivid and tender memories', but with a different purpose. Now in his thirties, and captivated by the new science of photography, Frith set out on a series of pioneering journeys to the Nile regions that occupied him from 1856 until 1860.

Intrigue and Adventure

He took with him on his travels a specially-designed wicker carriage that acted as both dark-room and sleeping chamber. These far-flung journeys were packed with intrigue and adventure. In his life story, written when he was sixty-three, Frith tells of being held captive by bandits, and of fighting 'an awful midnight battle to the very point of surrender with a deadly pack of hungry, wild dogs'. Sporting flowing Arab costume, Frith arrived at Akaba by camel seventy years before Lawrence, where he encountered 'desert princes and rival sheikhs, blazing with jewel-hilted swords'.

During these extraordinary adventures he was assiduously exploring the desert regions bordering the Nile and patiently recording the antiquities and peoples with his camera. He was the first photographer to venture beyond the sixth cataract. Africa was still the mysterious 'Dark Continent', and Stanley and Livingstone's historic meeting was a decade into the future. The conditions for picture taking confound belief. He laboured for hours in his wicker dark-room in the sweltering heat of the desert, while the volatile chemicals fizzed dangerously in their trays. Often he was forced to work in remote tombs and caves where conditions were cooler. Back in London he exhibited his photographs and was 'rapturously cheered' by members of the Royal Society. His reputation as a photographer was made overnight. An eminent modern historian has likened their impact on the population of the time to that on our own generation of the first photographs taken on the surface of the moon.

Venture of a Life-Time

Characteristically, Frith quickly spotted the opportunity to create a new business as a specialist publisher of photographs. He lived in an era of immense and sometimes violent change. For the poor in the early part of Victoria's reign work was a drudge and the hours long, and people had precious little free time to enjoy themselves. Most had no transport other than a cart or gig at their disposal, and had not travelled far beyond the boundaries of their own town or village. However,

by the 1870s, the railways had threaded their way across the country, and Bank Holidays and half-day Saturdays had been made obligatory by Act of Parliament. All of a sudden the ordinary working man and his family were able to enjoy days out and see a little more of the world.

With characteristic business acumen, Francis Frith foresaw that these new tourists would enjoy having souvenirs to commemorate their days out. In 1860 he married Mary Ann Rosling and set out with the intention of photographing every city, town and village in Britain. For the next thirty years he travelled the country by train and by pony and trap, producing fine photographs of seaside resorts and beauty spots that were keenly bought by millions of Victorians. These prints were painstakingly pasted into family albums and pored over during the dark nights of winter, rekindling precious memories of summer excursions.

The Rise of Frith & Co

Frith's studio was soon supplying retail shops all over the country. To meet the demand he gathered about him a small team of photographers, and published the work of independent artist-photographers of the calibre of Roger Fenton and Francis Bedford. In order to gain some understanding of the scale of Frith's business one only has to look at the catalogue issued by Frith & Co in 1886: it runs to some 670 pages, listing not only many thousands of views of the British Isles but also many photographs of most European countries, and China, Japan, the USA and Canada – note the sample page shown above from the hand-written *Frith & Co* ledgers detailing pictures taken. By 1890 Frith had created the greatest specialist photographic publishing company in the world,

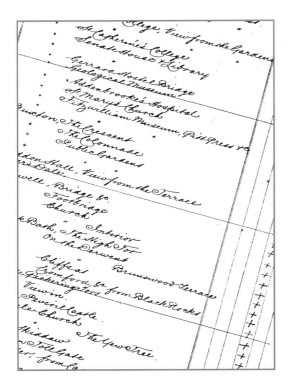

with over 2,000 outlets – more than the combined number that Boots and WH Smith have today! The picture on the right shows the *Frith & Co* display board at Ingleton in the Yorkshire Dales. Beautifully constructed with mahogany frame and gilt inserts, it could display up to a dozen local scenes.

Postcard Bonanza

The ever-popular holiday postcard we know today took many years to develop. In 1870 the Post Office issued the first plain cards, with a pre-printed stamp on one face. In 1894 they allowed other publishers' cards to be sent through the mail with an attached adhesive halfpenny stamp. Demand grew rapidly, and in 1895 a new size of postcard was permitted called the court card, but there was little room for illustration. In 1899, a year after Frith's death, a new card measuring 5.5 x 3.5 inches became the standard format, but it was not until 1902 that the divided back came into being, with address and message on one face and a full-size illustration on the other. *Frith & Co* were in the vanguard of postcard development, and Frith's sons Eustace and Cyril continued their father's monumental task, expanding the number of views offered to the public and recording more and more places in Britain, as the coasts and countryside were opened up to mass travel.

Francis Frith died in 1898 at his villa in Cannes, his great project still growing. The archive he created continued in business for another seventy years. By 1970 it contained over a third of a million pictures of 7,000 cities, towns and villages. The massive photographic record Frith has left to us stands as a living monument to a special and very remarkable man.

Frith's Archive: *A Unique Legacy*

FRANCIS FRITH'S legacy to us today is of immense significance and value, for the magnificent archive of evocative photographs he created provides a unique record of change in 7,000 cities, towns and villages throughout Britain over a century and more. Frith and his fellow studio photographers revisited locations many times down the years to update their views, compiling for us an enthralling and colourful pageant of British life and character.

We tend to think of Frith's sepia views of Britain as nostalgic, for most of us use them to conjure up memories of places in our own lives with which we have family associations. It often makes us forget that to Francis Frith they were records of daily life as it was actually being lived in the cities, towns and villages of his day. The Victorian age was one of great and often bewildering change for ordinary people, and though the pictures evoke an impression of slower times, life was as busy and hectic as it is today.

We are fortunate that Frith was a photographer of the people, dedicated to recording the minutiae of everyday life. For it is this sheer wealth of visual data, the painstaking chronicle of changes in dress, transport, street layouts, buildings, housing, engineering and landscape that captivates us so much today. His remarkable images offer us a powerful link with the past and with the lives of our ancestors.

Today's Technology

Computers have now made it possible for Frith's many thousands of images to be accessed almost instantly. In the Frith archive today, each photograph is carefully 'digitised' then stored on a CD Rom. Frith archivists can locate a single photograph amongst thousands within seconds. Views can be catalogued and sorted under a variety of categories of place and content to the immediate benefit of researchers.

Inexpensive reference prints can be created for them at the touch of a mouse button, and a wide range of books and other printed materials assembled and published for a wider, more general readership - in the next twelve months over a hundred Frith local history titles will be published! The day-to-day workings of the archive are very different from how they were in Francis Frith's time: imagine the herculean task of sorting through eleven tons of glass negatives as Frith had to do to locate a particular sequence of pictures! Yet

See Frith at www.francisfrith.co.uk

the archive still prides itself on maintaining the same high standards of excellence laid down by Francis Frith, including the painstaking cataloguing and indexing of every view.

It is curious to reflect on how the internet now allows researchers in America and elsewhere greater instant access to the archive than Frith himself ever enjoyed. Many thousands of individual views can be called up on screen within seconds on one of the Frith internet sites, enabling people living continents away to revisit the streets of their ancestral home town, or view places in Britain where they have enjoyed holidays. Many overseas researchers welcome the chance to view special theme selections, such as transport, sports, costume and ancient monuments.

We are certain that Francis Frith would have heartily approved of these modern developments in imaging techniques, for he himself was always working at the very limits of Victorian photographic technology.

The Value of the Archive Today

Because of the benefits brought by the computer, Frith's images are increasingly studied by social historians, by researchers into genealogy and ancestory, by architects, town planners, and by teachers and schoolchildren involved in local history projects.

In addition, the archive offers every one of us an opportunity to examine the places where we and our families have lived and worked down the years. Highly successful in Frith's own era, the archive is now, a century and more on, entering a new phase of popularity.

The Past in Tune with the Future

Historians consider the Francis Frith Collection to be of prime national importance. It is the only archive of its kind remaining in private ownership and has been valued at a million pounds. However, this figure is now rapidly increasing as digital technology enables more and more people around the world to enjoy its benefits.

Francis Frith's archive is now housed in an historic timber barn in the beautiful village of Teffont in Wiltshire. Its founder would not recognize the archive office as it is today. In place of the many thousands of dusty boxes containing glass plate negatives and an all-pervading odour of photographic chemicals, there are now ranks of computer screens. He would be amazed to watch his images travelling round the world at unimaginable speeds through network and internet lines.

The archive's future is both bright and exciting. Francis Frith, with his unshakeable belief in making photographs available to the greatest number of people, would undoubtedly approve of what is being done today with his lifetime's work. His photographs, depicting our shared past, are now bringing pleasure and enlightenment to millions around the world a century and more after his death.

Warwick - *An Introduction*

WARWICK is situated in the heart of England. Its origins lie some 5000 years ago in Neolithic times. After that date, nothing much is known about the town until the arrival of the Saxons. Whilst the Fosse Way lies close by, there is no evidence to show that the Romans came to Warwick. When the Saxons arrived on the scene, they settled by the River Avon. The river had its advantages, but it also provided a route for the Danes to travel and sack the town, as they did on at least four occasions.

A degree of peace came to the area with the arrival in 914 of Ethelfleda, daughter of Alfred the Great. Under her guidance a castle was built, and the growing town prospered. 1068 saw the arrival of the Normans and the beginnings of Warwick Castle as we know it today. However, Ethelfleda's Mound in the castle has nothing to do with her - it was a Victorian invention.

One man who made quite an impact on the town was Thomas Oken, who died childless in 1573. A wealthy merchant and burgess of Warwick, he set up a charity providing almshouses, which still operates today; he also endowed a schoolmaster. Under his instructions, an annual feast is held in his name: Oken's Feast, as it is called, originally cost 6d - it now costs much more. During the evening various speeches are made; for those who are invited to make a speech, this can be quite a daunting prospect. Thomas was the Guildmaster of the Religious Guild at the time of Henry VIII's Dissolution of the Monasteries. In order to thwart Henry's plans as far as Warwick was concerned, Thomas transferred the Guildhall to the town burgesses, who were the equivalent of the town council. The building is now part of the Lord Leycester Hospital.

1694 was a momentous year in Warwick's history. During the afternoon of 5 September, a serious fire started which was to destroy a vast area of the town. Luckily no person was killed, but many houses and their outbuildings were destroyed, along with several animals. An early casualty was the town fire engine. After it had burnt, human bucket chains were formed, and several houses were pulled down to form firebreaks. Another casualty was the old St Mary's church, but thanks to a concerted effort by the fire fighters, the Beauchamp Chapel was saved. Most of the buildings were constructed from timber and thatch, and were huddled close together; these factors, and a prevailing wind, meant that they did not take long to burn. Such fires in towns at this time were not uncommon. They were followed by a re-building scheme which empowered Commissioners to dictate the height of the new buildings, the materials used and so on. Financial inducements were available to encourage quick re-building, and likewise, financial penalties were available to discourage delays.

Warwick's other serious fire occurred in 1871 at the castle, and caused extensive damage. The castle staff could not cope, and needed assistance from nearby towns. This was easier said than done, as it was the week-end and the telegraph offices were closed, so mounted messengers were despatched. Some fire engines arrived the next day by railway from places such as Birmingham, over 20 miles away.

During the 18th century, the Earls of Warwick began moving some of their boundaries and encroached into the town. For instance, most of the wall in Castle Lane and the lodge originated at this time. Towards the end of the century, the old bridge into town fell into disrepair. The Earl offered to contribute 75% of the cost of a new bridge, and the council accepted his offer; the bridge was opened in 1793 and cost the Earl £3000. Both Bridge End and Mill Street were transformed into quiet backwaters. Soon after the new bridge was opened, the old one collapsed, and remains in a ruinous state today.

Developments in recent years have seen the castle move out of private ownership and become part of the Madame Tussaud's Group. The new market place provides a large open-air venue for events in addition to the weekly markets, but it has yet to meet its full potential. The demand for housing is ever increasing, although retail development is much slower.

Yet other traditions remain steadfast. The annual Mop Fair still arrives in October; it is a reminder of the old Mop Hiring Fairs, when people seeking employment put themselves up for hire, carrying the tools of their trade. For example, a maid might carry a mop - hence the fair's name. The following week was the Runaway Mop, which gave employees and employers a second chance if the previous week had not been to their mutual satisfaction. Whatever the result, the Mop Fairs were an excuse for celebrating, just as they are today. However, not everybody likes the idea of the town centre being taken oven by a funfair.

Another strong link with the past is Warwick`s Court Leet, which is one of only four in this part of the country. These Court Leets are the modern-day version of the old Manorial courts, and the jurymen and women report on the state of the footpaths, the road signs and so on. One of the more onerous tasks is undertaken by the Ale Taster, who is obliged to sample several of the ales being sold in the town to see if they are fit for human consumption. It is terrible work, but someone has to do it! At least he can taste the ale in modern civilised ways, rather than by using the traditional method of sitting in it.

The Approaches into Warwick

King's School 1892 31034s

The school was originally founded by Edward the Confessor and
sited in the town centre; John Cundall rebuilt it here in 1879.
Although the school continues to expand, it retains several
traditions. One is the annual visit of the Town Crier, who conveys
greetings from the Mayor and then awards 'a half-day respite from
their labours' to those 'who are deserving of it'. The front is floodlit
at night, and is beautifully reflected in the River Avon which flows
nearby. Old boys of the school include the poet John Masefield.

The New Bridge 1892 31013s

Consisting of a grand single-span arch 25ft high and 36ft wide, the bridge was built in 1790 by the Warwick architect William Eborall. He used stone from near-by Rock Mill in Leamington, which was conveyed to the site by boat. It cost £4000 - the town paid a quarter, and the Earl of Warwick found the balance. Sadly, there is no inscription on the bridge. It changed the whole approach into Warwick from the south, and resulted in a new road being made. There is a superb view of the castle from here.

The Old Bridge 1892 31011

Before the New Bridge was built, this was the only access from the south across the river. Consisting of 14 arches, the bridge crossed from Bridge End to Mill Street. Soon after the New Bridge was opened, this one collapsed, and it has remained a ruin ever since. There is no record if it having ever been a toll bridge, so the old stocks in Mill Street were for other wrongdoers. The access from Banbury was altered and went straight up to the East Gate instead of into Smith Street.

◀ **Bridge End c1955** W31053
This is a close-up of the view shown in 72355, taken approximately 25 years later. A new house, albeit in sympathetic style, has been added where a large garden used to be. Although some foliage has been removed, plenty has been left. Note the bootscraper in the porch, reminding us of the days when there were fewer pavements.

Bridge End 1922 72355
This cluster of cottages lies at the end of the old bridge. Once looked down upon by town residents, it is now a much sought-after part of Warwick. With the opening of the New Bridge, this suddenly became a tranquil unhurried area - it retains the feel of a small hamlet.

Bridge End c1950 W31052
There is a lack of activity in this gentle, quiet, sunny view, apart from the man in front of the car. He appears to be pulling a trolley of sorts. The car has a Coventry registration number, so it might belong to a visitor.

West Street c1955 W31086b
Before the opening of the by-pass, this was the main route through Warwick from Stratford and the west. As car ownership grew, it experienced much congestion at weekends, especially in the summer. St James's Chapel is situated on the old West Gate, and is part of the Lord Leycester Hospital. The hill is steeper than it looks, which used to be a problem for horse-drawn vehicles in winter. Local boys could earn a few pence by helping to pull horses up into town. Contrary to current trends, the pedestrian crossing has been removed.

▼ **Guy's Cliff Mill 1922** 72373

The Domesday Book records the first known mill on this site, probably not this particular one, which has been a longstanding tourist attraction. The balcony was added in 1821, otherwise the stone-built mill has changed very little. Running past the mill is a footpath to Old Milverton. The wall backing on to the river is a popular seat.

▼ **Guy's Cliff House Avenue 1922** 72372s

Begun in 1751, Guy's Cliff House was added to later, before becoming a ruin in the mid 20th century. Considerable fire damage was caused whilst a Sherlock Holmes film was being shot here some years ago - the building had to be restored to the ruined state it was in before the fire! A former housemaid, Sarah Kemble, eloped from here one morning and married her sweetheart William. She took to the stage and became the famous actress Sarah Siddons. In later years she became a welcome guest in the house where she had once been a maid.

Guy's Cliff House 1922 72371

On this site lived the legendary Saxon hero, Guy of Warwick. To prove his love for Phyllis, daughter of the Earl of Warwick, he spent years killing dangerous animals and men. Suffering from remorse for all these deaths, he returned to Warwick unbeknown to Phyllis and lived as a hermit. Not recognising her beloved, Phyllis tended him until he died. Only then did she realise whom she had been nursing. Unable to live without him, she too died. One story says she jumped into the river and drowned, whilst another version records that she pined away with a broken heart.

Guy's Cliff Mill c1955
W31026
The mill looks run down here, but soon after this photograph was taken it was joined to the miller's house and turned into a restaurant, known as the Saxon Mill. The mill wheel has been replaced, and a glass panel has been installed for the diners to watch the water flowing past. Marks on the wall inside serve as reminders of the flood levels recorded over the years.

The River Avon and Mill Street

The Castle from the River 1892 30997
This has long been one of the most photographed
scenes in England, and it is a view which does not
change very much. At the time of this photograph,
the land to the right had yet to be converted into
tennis courts for the Boat Club. The foliage shows
that this is a summer's day. The area was flooded as
recently as 1998.

◄ **Mill Street c1955** W31059d
It was at about the time of this photograph when the Mill Street residents purchased their homes from the Earl of Warwick. The street is an architectural paradise, with buildings of various styles and ages. Those on the left have to contend with some occasional flooding from the river. Whilst having the castle as a neighbour does cause problems, the residents are handily placed for enjoying the open-air concerts and fireworks displays from the comfort of their own gardens.

The Castle from the Bridge 1922 72366
It is 30 years after 30997 (pages 22-23) and the land to the right is much more tended. The man in the punt adds a touch of tranquillity to a typical timeless scene from rural England. Although messing about in boats was very much a Victorian pastime, clearly it had not yet died out.

Mill Street 1922 72351
Just past the last house on the left, by the trees, is Arthur Measures' Garden, which is one of Warwick's treasures. It goes down to the river, with close-up views of the castle and the old bridge. The whole area is popular for wedding photographs, and it is not uncommon to find wedding cars queuing up for their turn.

Old Cottages 1892 31032
Two years after this picture was taken, the nearby mill began supplying electricity to the castle. The equipment was water-driven, and if there was not enough, it could be supplemented by using gas. When this happened, the Mill Street residents suffered a significant reduction of gas pressure.

Mill Street 1922 72353
One offshoot of the castle's electricity supply was the acquisition of an electric-powered car and river launch. The car only had one seat, so the poor instructor had to run alongside. Mystery surrounds the methods used to train the launch operators.

The Castle, Caesar's Tower 1892 31006
The tower has no connection with Julius Caesar or with any Roman emperor. It was originally named Poitiers Tower, after the Bishop of Poitiers, who was captured during the Hundred Years War. His ransom paid for the tower, which is situated at the bottom of Mill Street. Its angled base and curved walls would have made climbing a scaling ladder a risky business.

St John's and Smith Street

▶ St John's 1892 31031
The two houses behind the pump (left) have flying freeholds, whereby the bedroom of one house is over the living room of the other. Next to them is the site of the County Cinema, evoking memories of Saturday children's cinema clubs. There was always a cliffhanger which was never quite the same when the story resumed the following week.

▼ St John's House 1892 31028s
The house was built around 1626 on the site of the 12th-century Hospital of St John. It now houses the County and Royal Warwickshire Regiment of Fusiliers museums. During the 18th and 19th centuries, the building was a school for educating young ladies. A fully-equipped Victorian schoolroom is available for modern children to experience the harshness of earlier education.

◀ **Smith Street c1955** W31059c
The trams have gone, and their cable holders have been converted into lamps. Occasionally traces of the old rails appear during roadworks. Outside the Tuck Shop Café is an old 'no entry' sign. The Roebuck (beyond the café) has changed from those days in the 1970s when you could watch your beef sandwich being carved and made up behind the bar.

East Gate and Landor House 1892 31029

The fine house on this side of East Gate was modernised in 1692, just two years before the Great Fire. Its owner, a Dr Johnson (not the Dr Johnson) was so concerned about the approach of the fire, that he had a neighbour's house demolished as a firebreak. Unfortunately, the fire went nowhere near his house, and he had to pay £20 in compensation. 1775 saw the birth here of the poet Walter Savage Landor, who tended to live up to his middle name. Today the house forms part of King's High School for Girls.

East Gate c1955 W31059b

Vehicles will continue to pass through the arch for a few more years. The road behind the car was built to accommodate the early trams; until it was completed, the open-top horse-drawn trams went through the arch. Regulations would not permit passengers to ride on top during this stage - but not everyone obeyed this rule! Beyond the sweet shop (left) is the former Castle Arms. One morning in March 1916, a tram ran away from outside the Warwick Arms and crashed into it: yet the bar clock continued ticking, and the mirror was not cracked. Only minor injuries were sustained.

The Town Centre

East Gate 1922 72349

Electric trams were introduced in 1905. The building next to the
Porridge Pot (left) is a 14th-century hall house with a Victorian
mock-Tudor front. The Porridge Pot housed tea rooms that have
been frequented by many, including pupils from Warwick
School. Until July 2002 an old cauldron hung there as a sign.
The place is now an Italian restaurant, with a new sign which
does not enhance this lovely old building. Before the traffic
lights were installed, an RAC patrolman was employed to
direct traffic.

► East Gate and Jury Street 1892 31030
The two girls on the left stand beside the entrance to the Lord Leycester Hotel, which was the eastern extent of the fire. On the other side of the street is a superb timber-fronted building - the ornate woodwork demonstrates the wealth of its original owners.

◄ East Gate 1922 72349c
This is another part of Warwick which does not change - the two-step kerb still exists. Hats and caps seem to be the order of the day, except for the little girl in the pushchair. How strange to see young boys wearing their caps with the peaks pointing forwards!

◀ **Jury Street c1950** W31042
The trams have gone, and
the cable holders make
attractive lampposts. Just by
the Porridge Pot is an old-
fashioned pedestrian
crossing without the stripes
on the road surface. The
traffic lights at East Gate are
now installed.

High Street 1922

72343

The Warwick Arms area is always a busy part of the town. In the hotel's heyday, there was stabling for 70 horses at the rear. The glass canopy has now gone, but the bunch of grapes above remains. Driving on the left does not seem to apply in Warwick! The 'all cars stop here sign' (centre right) is a tram stop, and the cables are still visible. Opposite is Thacker and Christmas's grocery shop - allegedly unsafe, it was demolished. The site now houses an antiques centre and offices.

◄ **Corn Market 1922** 72356s
There has been little change in the
30 years since 31033 was taken.
The carved head over the doorway,
known as Old Tom, later had to be
raised to avoid continuous damage
by high-sided vehicles in the late
20th century and the ground floor
windows were to be converted into
modern shop fronts.

◀ **The Shakespeare Restaurant 1892** 31033
The original house was built in 1634 and escaped the fire. The intricate woodwork all round this building indicates wealth. Today the building houses Lunn Poly travel agents. This is the era of shop sunblinds; they had to be high enough to allow a policemen to walk underneath without losing his helmet.

◀ **St Mary's Church 1892** 31015
This view looks almost the same today. Regardless of the change of owners, the street remains a mixture of business and residential properties. Very few have off-street parking, which was not a problem in 1892. The stone building on the right is still called the Athenaeum; the local gentry used it as a club during the 19th century.

Church Street 1922

72345

The trees have thickened in the churchyard, and the war memorial has been erected. Its site is appropriate, for it stands at the end of the railings where casualty notices were posted during World War I.

Church Street 1922 72346

St Mary's church dominates this part of town. It was rebuilt after the fire by Sir William Wilson from Leicester - Christopher Wren's plans were not chosen. During the Middle Ages, St Mary's amassed a collection of holy relics which have since disappeared. The church office is the last house on the left; it was a Froebel School between the wars. There is an excellent view from the tower, from which one can see those town centre buildings which still retain gardens instead of parking areas.

Church Street c1960

W31036

Where is all the traffic? The Zetland Arms Hotel (left) is now well established. In the 1970s it was home to Casey, an elderly Labrador dog, who had a very good relationship with the butchers in the town. When he died, the local newspaper published his photograph complete with an obituary.

St Mary's Church from the Jetty c1955 W31059a
Looking up towards St Mary's from here, we get a good impression of how close the timber-framed buildings were in 1694, creating an immediate fire hazard. The large sign on the left behind the lamppost belongs to the Gold Cup. Behind it is the Aylesford Hotel, the first house to be re-built after the fire.

St Mary's Church

St Mary's Church 1892 31016

Northgate Street was a fashionable part of town, in spite of being opposite the Assize (now Crown) Court and the gaol. The houses are now offices in differing states of repair. One of the church carillons is 'Warwickshire Lads and Lassies', which always raises a cheer when it is played by military bands. It was the regiment march for the Royal Warwickshire.

St Mary's Church, the Interior looking East 1892 31019
The upper side galleries have gone, and so have the box pews. A new pulpit donated by the Freemasons was moved to the right-hand side of the church some years ago. Amongst the memorials in the chancel is one to William Parr, brother of Henry VIII's last wife. He died suddenly in Warwick, and Queen Elizabeth I paid for his funeral.

St Mary's Church, the Beauchamp Chapel 1892 31021
The Beauchamp Chapel is probably one of the finest burial chambers in England. The central figure is Richard Beauchamp, Earl of Warwick, lying underneath a cage called a herse, which was meant to support a fabric cover. He oversaw the execution of Joan of Arc. Undoubtedly concerned for what might happen to his soul, he had this chapel built. It took 21 years and cost over £2783, an incredible amount in those days, approximately £1,750,000 by today's values. Masses were to be said here for him 3 times a day. Fortunately the chapel was saved from the fire, thanks to the efforts of local people.

The Lord Leycester Hospital

The Lord Leycester Hospital 1892 31022
St James's Chapel is situated over the West Gate (left), once known as the hanging gate. Visitors were charged a toll for entering the town, and here convicted felons were hanged. The chapel was renovated in the 19th century by Sir George Gilbert Scott; it contains work by William Morris, a leading member of the Arts and Crafts Movement.

High Street 1922 72359c
This is a close-up detail of
72359; the general shop sells
refreshments and souvenirs.
The third postcard down on
the right appears to be of
West Gate and the Lord
Leycester Hospital. It would
be interesting to see what
other views there are, and if
any are by Francis Frith!

Westgate and the Lord Leycester Hospital 1922 72359

Looking down West Street reminds us that Warwick is a hill town. By the archway is one of the town's two Victorian post boxes, introduced in 1856. The vertical slot was not popular, as it let in the rain. The low building on the right once made soda water and has become a shop.

The Lord Leycester Hospital 1892 31025

The timber-framing is coloured naturally, and is not Victorian chocolate-box black and white. Luckily the buildings survived the fire, which started almost opposite. The porch dates from the 17th century, and was the entrance to the Anchor Inn. The white building to the right is the old Bear and Baculus Inn.

The Lord Leycester Hospital c1955 W31033

It is 30 years after 72359, and a few changes have taken place. The shop is now part of the Hospital. Cyclists are visiting, and there is a remarkable lack of traffic for 9.45am. In the top right-hand corner is the sign for the Bear and Baculus (Latin for stick), which is just another name for the Bear and Ragged Staff, the coat of arms of the Earls of Warwick.

▼ The Lord Leycester Hospital c1890 W31399

If you are thinking how nice a hospital this looks for your treatment, then think again! This is not a hospital in today's terminology, but more of a hostel. In reality, it is a collection of buildings. Originally it was used by the religious Guild of St George and the Blessed Virgin until the reign of Henry VIII. The buildings were saved from Henry's depravations by Thomas Oken, who transferred them to the town's burgesses. This is another summertime picture - the pet bird in its cage above the entrance is enjoying the sunshine.

▼ The Lord Leycester Hospital 1892 31023

In 1571, Robert Dudley, Earl of Leicester and favourite of Queen Elizabeth I, acquired the Hospital to house twelve of his retired retainers. The burgesses were evicted and moved into what is now the Court House. Not surprisingly, there was little opposition to Leicester's plan. Locally his name is always spelt Leycester.

▲ The Lord Leycester Hospital 1922 72360s

A few years ago the Master had the buildings re-tiled, and there was an immediate outcry about them looking too new. It is said that the remedy was to have the tiles sprayed with animal waste matter. True story or otherwise, the criticism soon ceased!

◀ **The Lord Leycester Hospital, the Quadrangle 1892** 31026
The main building is the Master's House, which, at first glance, is a superb timber-framed Tudor building. In fact the front is Victorian, added because of the bad state of repair of the original. On it are carvings of several groups of bears, who look as if they are playing musical instruments in a 1950s skiffle group.

The Lord Leycester Hospital 1922 72361s
The archway to the right leads into the courtyard. To its left is the entrance into the Great Hall. James I was entertained here in 1617; the banquet in his honour cost so much money that the town was still paying for it 10 years later. The steps lead up to St James's Chapel.

The Lord Leycester Hospital, the Courtyard 1922 72363
The bear and ragged staff figures proudly on the Master's House and faces the blue porcupine of the Stanley family. The other shields are the coats of arms of families associated with the Dudleys. Sixty years ago, admission to the Lord Leycester was 6d, but cameras had to pay 1s.

The Lord Leycester Hospital 1922 72362
Unfortunately, the upstairs gallery to the left is currently roped off as being unsafe. This may be the result of a photocall in 2001 when some twenty town criers and their escorts stood there during their Warwick bi-annual competition organised by the Court Leet. The gallery has never been the same since then!

Warwick Castle

The Castle
Guy's and Caesar's Towers 1892 31000a

This approach was designed in the 18th century so that the castle
would be very impressive for visitors arriving up the drive; it still has
that effect for visitors today. The ticket office is in the stables block -
and the front driveway tends to be used mainly for special events.
Guy's Tower is to the right. To the left is the Victorian Rose Garden
opened by the late Princess of Wales.

The Castle Entrance 1892 31007
The ivy has long since been cleared. Going through the entrance, we get some idea of how high the bridge is across the river. As the main entrance, this would have been defended very strongly. The castle has been used for shooting films such as 'The Black Rose' and 'Prince Valiant'.

▶ **The Castle, the Portcullis c1900**
W31301
Should any attacker pass through the first portcullis, he would find another one behind. At the same time he would face a lethal cross-fire of missiles, including those dropped or shot through holes in the ceiling. These weapon slits are well named 'murder holes'. Such attackers were often referred to as 'the forlorn hope', as they had little chance of surviving.

▼ **The Castle, in the Courtyard 1892** 31008
Peacocks (right) are part of the Castle's heritage, although they do not wander around the town like they once did. Newcomers to the town, especially those living close to the castle, do not always take kindly to their noise. Local lore maintains that if you hear the peacocks cry, then it means rain - and it usually does.

▲ **The Castle, in the Courtyard 1892** 31009
The courtyard hosts the annual lantern-lit carol service in December. Over 3000 people gather in the dark, nearly all carrying lanterns, for an evening of carol singing. Hot punch, soup and chestnuts are available. Beginning in the 1970s, the tradition is still carried on, and let us hope it will do so for many more years to come. Originally there were coke braziers for extra warmth, but these have had to go on safety grounds. It must be quite a sight to see from the air. One year, during the Nativity Play, one of the angel's wings caught fire!

◀ **The Castle Courtyard c1950** W31633b
Clearly this was taken before the arrival of any visitors, probably from Ethelfleda's Mound. The castle remains in such good condition because it never really came under siege; the Earls tended to keep on the winning side, although they did not always survive themselves.

The Castle, the Great Hall c1900 W31302
The fire of 1871 resulted in considerable damage to the castle, including the Great Hall. It was rebuilt by Anthony Salvin, who also worked on the Tower of London. Today's Great Hall would almost be unrecognisable from this photograph. The foliage has gone, and the hall has been opened out. At Christmas it is decorated, and has a huge tree in one corner. The hall is available for hire for private functions. It has an excellent collection of suits of armour and a cauldron the old Porridge Pot would have been proud to own.

The Castle, the Drawing Room c1900 W31304
This room's cedar panelling was completed in the late 17th century by Roger and William Harbutt. Later, Roger would be involved in work at Landor House in Smith Street. There is a distinct Italian feel to the room, which is enhanced by a magnificent plastered ceiling.

The Castle, the Drawing Room c1900 W31303
Here we see typical Victorian clutter, which is absolutely fine if you have an army of servants to do the cleaning. This would not have been a problem in the castle. By 1900 the room would have electric light; although this was perhaps not too efficient, it was a good way to impress visitors.

The Castle 1892 31005
The small building adjoining the water-wheel is the old mill, which was opened to the public in early 2002. It first produced electricity for the castle two years after this photograph was taken, making it one of the first great homes to do so. The event was commemorated by a sumptuous ball in the castle later in 1894.

Round and About Warwick

Charlecote Park

Charlecote Park has been in the hands of the Lucy family since 1189 until it was taken over by the National Trust in the 1940s. The grounds were laid out by Lancelot Capability Brown in 1766.

Charlecote Park, from the Upper Gardens c1884 17112
The broad gatehouse gives the impression of being Elizabethan, although it is largely Victorian. In the stables are several horse-drawn carriages, including the ones used by the family for their grand tours in the 1800s.

▲ **Charlecote Park c1955** C25101
The house was burgled in 1854 by two of the most inept criminals who ever plotted crime in Warwickshire. They left a trail of clues behind them which anyone could have followed. They were soon arrested in Birmingham, and most of the property was recovered.

◀ **Charlecote Park, the Great Hall c1890** C2512305
The stag's head is a reminder of the local legend about William Shakespeare poaching deer in the grounds. Later he lampooned Sir Thomas Lucy as Mr Justice Shallow, who told tales of his youth to Falstaff. The lamp is of the rise and fall variety, and would have held oil or gas. Electricity was not installed until the mid 20th century.

Claverdon

The village is on the main Warwick to Redditch road, and is not very far from Henley-in-Arden. Mentioned in the Domesday Book, its name is derived from Early English and means 'clover hill'. There is a monument in the church to Thomas Spencer, who was an ancestor of the late Princess of Wales. A more illustrious memorial is to Sir Francis Galton, who was a cousin of Charles Darwin. His claim to fame is the development of crime detection by the use of fingerprints.

▲ **Claverdon, The Forge c1955** C253022a
The horseshoe shape of the doorway is a clue to the building's original use. It is not used as a forge today, but houses Sparkes Chimneys and Stoves. The window shutters remain, and the only new addition is a brick-mounted post box to the right. The box is from the reign of George VI, erected after his death.

◄ **Claverdon, The Country Stores and the Post Office c1955** C253022c
This business has since moved nearer to Warwick into a pretty thatched-roofed building. The old stores are now a private house. The post box has gone, but otherwise there have been very few changes.

Henley-in-Arden

Black's 1881 Guide to Warwickshire describes Henley as 'a quaint, straggly old place', which is an apt description. One suggestion for the meaning of its name is quite simply 'an old place in the Forest of Arden'. The town's main street is about one mile long, and enjoys a wealth of different architectural styles.

Some years ago the manor of Henley-in-Arden was purchased by an American, Joseph Hardy. Contrary to the worries of many people, he has spent money on the town. One of his projects was the setting up of the Heritage Centre, next to the Tudor Dairies. The building contains a vast amount of information on Henley and its inhabitants, both past and present.

Henley sits astride the old A34 Birmingham to Oxford Road. Nearby is the M40, which is a far cry from the pre-mechanised age of transport.

▼ **Henley-in-Arden, View from the Mount c1950** H414011
At one time Henley had a large castle, which has long since gone. However, it was excavated during a recent Time Team programme on Channel 4. In the 17th century, inhabitants of Henley were described as being 'vain and idle persons who spent time erecting a maypole'.

▲ **Henley-in-Arden, The Market Cross c1955**
H414007
There have been very many changes to this seemingly timeless scene. The Market Cross is a reminder of the days when a bargain was sealed under the binding shadow of a cross. Farmers' wives came to market to sell small items to enable them to buy pins and other needlework necessities, hence the expression 'pin money.'

Henley-in-Arden, High Street 1949 H414015
St John the Baptist's church was begun in the 15th century. It is a church of convenience, as it does not have a graveyard attached. Also begun in the 15th century was the Guild Hall, built by Sir Ralph Boteler. It is now home to the Henley Court Leet.

Henley-in-Arden, High Street 1949 H414008
One of the more appealing buildings in Henley is the White Swan (centre right), which was a well-known coaching inn. It stands on the long road between Birmingham and Oxford and provided sustenance for weary travellers. According to local legend, Charles II called here in disguise when fleeing from his defeat at Worcester in 1651.

Henley-in-Arden, The Yews 1959 H414032
On the left, by the first car, is the famous Tudor Dairies Ice Creamery, which started up in 1934. By 1938 it had become so popular that traffic control was necessary. Production suffered during the Second World War, and peacetime restrictions and food rationing meant that ice cream was available only on Wednesday and Saturday afternoon. For a youngster brought up on wartime austerity, it was a treat not to be missed. There then followed a mixed career for the Dairies before it returned to private ownership. Harry and Arthur Fathers, who founded the business, would be amazed at the flavours of ice cream now available.

Kenilworth

The town has Saxon origins: a Kenelph or Kenelm had a 'worthe', or dwelling-place here. The castle's origins go back to the days of Henry I. King John was a regular visitor, and the castle reverted to the Crown. To be fair, John spent money on its upkeep. During the Baronial Wars which followed his reign, the castle was besieged, holding out for over six months before negotiating an honourable surrender. In later years Queen Elizabeth was another regular royal visitor. One such visit cost £60,000, which was a vast amount of money in those days. The modern town of today is still a long straggling street showing signs of much re-development. On the other hand, the Old Town is still a delight. Not having had a railway station since the Dr Beeching closures of the 1960s, Kenilworth is now on track to have a new one built. However, the move is not very popular with those most likely to be affected by it, as can be imagined.

Kenilworth
The Castle Green c1960 K5047

The Queen and Castle (right) now belongs to the Beefeater Group, and the illuminated AA and RAC signs have gone. The creepers remain, and so does the old-style telephone kiosk (centre). The tea rooms behind it have gone. An old-style coach, on the left, is leaving the car park, where the hunt used to meet on Boxing Day. The duck race and other entertainments inside the castle have replaced it. Ubiquitous double yellow lines have replaced the 'no waiting' sign opposite the coach.

▶ **Kenilworth, The Castle 1892** 30935
The castle became one of the casualties of the English Civil War when it was pulled down by Cromwell's supporters. Now these romantic ruins are cared for by English Heritage. The ivy was removed in the 1930s. Each Boxing Day morning the ruins and grounds are open for visitors until midday. Then the Warwick Town Crier calls from the towers at closing time, advising visitors of the perils of being locked in overnight! So far his warnings have been heeded. Queen Elizabeth I conferred the castle on her favourite, Robert Dudley.

▼ Kenilworth, High Street c1955 K5022

If we continue down this street, we come into the Old Town. The main changes that have happened since this photograph are the volume of traffic, the parking restrictions and the growth of television aerials. Also, the telegraph pole has moved to the other side of the street.

◀ Kenilworth, From below the Footbridge 1892 30941

The ford has long been prone to flooding, and a common sight was the abandoned motors of drivers who did not heed the warnings. One such driver ignored the advice of a local police officer, and found himself and his passengers stranded. They were all in evening dress, and had to wade through the water in all their finery. The officer was unsympathetic, and the driver's passengers were not at all pleased with their chauffeur! Nearby is the start of the duck race, which can be quite risky when the stream is in spate.

Kenilworth
The Bank and the Post Office 1892 30949

This building still stands, but with some alterations and the removal of
its name. Downstairs is the Bank Gallery, with offices on top. Ironically,
the current post office is almost opposite. The driveway to the right
leads down to the Norman doorway into St Nicholas's church.

Kineton

Before the Norman Conquest, Kineton was a royal domain and later home of King John. Kingstown is one suggestion of the origin of its name. This market town has many old stone buildings. Nearby is the site of the Battle of Edgehill, which was the first major encounter of the English Civil War in 1642. Little Kineton, sometimes known as Lower Kineton, is just outside the town, and once housed the kennels of the Warwickshire Hunt.

Kineton, Southam Street c1965 K65019
The buildings on the left are Anvil House and Forge House, which indicates one of their former uses. Behind the timber-framed Morris 1000 car, the Stores have reverted to private ownership, and the telegraph pole has gone. On the other side of the road is the Wesleyan Methodist Church, erected in 1893.

Kineton, Little Kineton c1965 K65025
This is a tranquil, rural scene which does not alter very much. Some of the posts and chain around the pond have been removed. The block of houses on the left has been altered, and new ones are being built behind. A telephone kiosk and post box are other newcomers on the scene.

Royal Leamington Spa

Black's 1881 'Guide to Warwickshire' described Leamington as 'pleasantly situated on the Leam, a tributary of the Avon'. Since its leap to prosperity in the early 19th century, Leamington has continued to grow right up to the present day. The older parts still have an air of graciousness about them. To a degree, areas in the most rundown areas of town still remind us of those far-off days.

Leamington has managed to change with the times. When the fashion for taking the waters ceased to be fashionable, the town changed tack. It made itself appealing to retired gentlefolk with army, naval, church, and colonial service backgrounds, and encouraged them to settle here. The idea worked. Prior to 1939, the ratio of elderly people to youngsters was 3:1. During the 1950s-1970s period this trend reversed, with a greater ratio of younger people. It is no longer the town for people to move to for retirement.

The planning battles between residents and developers continues to rage fiercely, and none more so than the battle over the future of the Regent Hotel. Industrial estates continue to grow alongside new housing developments. Who knows what the future will bring?

Leamington Spa, From the Tower of All Saints' 1922 72435
This is a wonderful bird's eye view, which makes Parade and Lower Parade easy to follow. To the left of the Town Hall campanile is the spire of St Alban's church, nicknamed the mouldy cheese spire, because it was covered in copper which turned green.

Leamington Spa, The River Leam 1892
30984
The town derives its name from the River Leam, which flows leisurely through it. This is clearly a summer's day, and the boys are relaxing with their trousers rolled up. No doubt they have been paddling or just dangling their feet in the water.

▼ **Leamington Spa, Spencer Street 1892** 30950
In the distance is All Saints' church and the now demolished Camden Well, which was the only source of spa water enjoyed by ordinary people. On the left is the former Congregational chapel, which was built in 1836 with four Ionic columns. It has just closed (2002) as a carpet warehouse. The iron railings have long since gone, probably as part of a scrap metal drive during the last war.

▼ **Leamington Spa, The Pump Room 1892** 30955
All self-respecting spa towns had to have a pump room, and Leamington was no exception. Opened in 1814, it has survived to the present day, though not without some difficulties. The turrets have been removed, and so have the iron railings; the swimming baths are now on the Campion Hills. It has only recently been re-opened, and is now home to the library, museum, and tourist information centre.

▲ **Leamington Spa, War Memorial Gardens 1922** 72446
On the right is Euston Place, home to most of the estate agents in the town. The Town Hall campanile is beyond them to the centre. Spring is a good time to see the flowers in the gardens, when they are alive with colour. How sad it is that there are more names on the War Memorial for victims of World War II, Korea, the Falklands and Northern Ireland.

◄ **Leamington Spa, Regent Grove 1892** 30959
The buildings on the left are shops, but the old theatre, behind the four lamps, has suffered the final indignity of being demolished and turned into a car park. The trees opposite formed part of a private driveway up to the Campion Hills.

Leamington Spa, Parade and the Town Hall 1892 30953
John Cundall's Tudor/Baroque-style Town Hall seems totally out of place in a Regency town. However, you cannot be indifferent to it - you either like it or loathe it! Since 1974 it has been owned by Warwick District Council, complete with its Assembly Room and municipal offices. Queen Victoria's statue was erected in 1904.

Long Itchington

The village has Roman origins, and was home to Wulfstan. Although not a well-educated man, he became a great statesman and helped compile the Domesday Book. He quickly swore allegiance to William the Conqueror, to whom he was fiercely loyal. Also, he was very loyal to William II. Wulfstan was a formidable character who had to fight to achieve success. His efforts helped to bring Normans and Saxons together.

Long Itchington, The Village c1955 L166007
The Commercial Inn (centre) is now called the Harvester, a more fitting reminder of the rural nature of Long Itchington. The area left of the Harvester has been rebuilt, and now includes a newsagent. Opposite, H Windsor has become a Country Store, and unlike its competitors in the village, closes on Sundays.

Long Itchington, The Village c1955 L166008
The grassy area has been tidied up, complete with kerbed edges. Facing us is the Malt House. The telegraph pole to its left has been moved to the other side, whilst the other pole has gone. The light-coloured building jutting out on the right is the Green Man public house, which currently shows exposed beams and is a yellow/cream colour.

Southam

Once thought to be a Saxon town, the discovery of Roman coins in the area has cast some doubt as to the date of its origin. The town's main claim to fame (or infamy, depending on your point of view), concerns its dealings with Charles I. He was unpopular in Southam, and the locals showed it. Another link with the past is the visits of the annual Mop Fairs, which take over the town centre.

Southam, The Old Mint c1960 S298038
The pub's unusual name came about as this was where Charles I had a mint at the time of the battle of Edgehill. He required all his followers to surrender their silver plate to be cast into coins to pay his troops. The building was re-furbished in 1996, and has a wealth of stonework and exposed beams.

Southam, Market Hill c1960 S298048
Notice the bricked-up windows (left), a legacy of the infamous window tax, where owners paid tax according to the number of glass windows in their buildings. It led to the expression 'daylight robbery', as windows were bricked up to reduce the amount of tax to be paid. The tax on glass was repealed just in time for the building of the Crystal Palace for the Great Exhibition of 1851.

◀ **Southam, The Manor House and Market Hill c1960** S298030
Little did the builder of the Manor House realise that it would be turned into a chemist's shop in the 20th century. Remember the days when petrol stations, or garages as they were known then, stood on the main streets? This one has become a Chinese takeaway. Further down the hill, the Craven Arms is now residential accommodation.

Southam, High Street c1960 S298033
When Charles I left Southam, the townspeople were glad to see him go. As a final insult, they refused to ring the church bells to speed him on his way. Totally enraged, he returned to the town and fined the inhabitants. He might have difficulty today in recognising the town with all its traffic.

Southam, Daventry Street c1960 S298037
This is another view of the old Manor House and pharmacy. On the right the Crown Inn, still keeping its name, has removed its rendering and exposed a mixture of natural stone and old beams. The raised pavement is still there.

Whitnash

Once a village on the outskirts of Royal Leamington Spa, Whitnash was only accessible by footpaths across the fields. It is now a town with its own mayor and council, and continues to grow. When the local tram service began, it was intended to include Whitnash, but it never did so. The town continues to grow. In the 17th century, Nicholas Greenhill became rector for 40 years, having been one of the youngest headmasters at Rugby School.

Whitnash, The Village 1922 72483
Looking at Whitnash from the church, we can see several changes. The shops on the left have gone - shopping is carried on elsewhere in town or at the local retail parks. The town enjoys a good road network, and no longer has to rely on footpaths across the fields.

Whitnash, St Margaret's Church 1922 72485
The church was restored during the 19th century by Sir George Gilbert Scott. Further additions and alterations have since followed. Steps were added to the war memorial in 1995 to celebrate 50 years of peace.

Whitnash, The Windmill c1960 W214015c
Once, this was Leamington's only surviving windmill, but now it has gone. A flourishing pub of the same name stands on the site, with a housing estate behind. Opposite from where this photograph was taken, is the site of some of Leamington's industry. An old Midland Red bus stop sign is by the side of the tree.

Wilmcote

This is a famous village, just outside Stratford and once the home of Mary Arden. She was the youngest of eight daughters, and married a certain John Shakespeare who took her to live in Stratford. One of their children was William Shakespeare.

Wilmcote
Mary Arden's House c1965 W216127

In fact, this is not Mary Arden's house, as had long been thought. By the year 2000 the mystery had been solved: her home is to the left, and out of sight of this photograph. The Shakespeare Birthplace Trust had long suspected that this was the wrong house, and arranged for the examination.

Acknowledgements

Black's Guide to Warwickshire 1881

William Field: The Town and Castle of Warwick

The Warwickshire Federation of Women's Institutes: The Warwickshire
Village Book

Arthur Mee: The King's England - Warwickshire

Nikolaus Pevsner and Alexandra Wedgwood: The Buildings of England -
Warwickshire

Ward Lock's Warwick and Shakespeare's Warwickshire

Edmund Bealby Wright: Sketch Book Guide - Warwick

Rosemary Booth: Warwick in old Picture Postcards

P J E Gates: Warwick in Times Past

Warwick Castle Guide Book

S Swingle and K Turner: The Warwick and Leamington Tramways

Chris Lines: The Book of Warwick

R K Morris and K Hoverd: The Buildings of Warwick

St Mary's Look Around the Collegiate Church

Collegiate Church of St Mary Guide Book

Graham Sutherland: Leamington Spa - A Photographic History of Your Town
(Francis Frith Collection)

Notes from The Warwick Society

Index

Bridge End 16-17

Castle 22-23, 24-25, 27, 52, 53, 54-55, 56, 57

Church Street 38-39, 40

Corn Market 36

East Gate 30, 31, 32-33

Guy's Cliff Avenue 18

Guy's Cliff House 18-19

Guy's Cliff Mill 18, 20-21

High Street 34-35

Jury Street 33

Landor's House 30

Lord Leycester Hospital 44-45, 46-47, 48-49, 50, 51

Mill Street 24, 25, 26

New Bridge 15

Old Bridge 15

River Avon 22-23

St John's 28-29

St John's House 28

St Mary's Church 37, 41, 42, 43

School 14

Shakespeare Restaurant 36-37

Smith Street 29

Westgate 46-47

West Street 17

Round and About Warwick

Charlecote Park 58-59, 60

Claverdon 61

Henley-in-Arden 62-63, 64

Kenilworth 65, 66-67, 68

Kineton 69

Long Itchington 78

Royal Leamington Spa 70-71, 72-73, 74-75, 76-77

Southam 79, 80-81

Whitnash 82-83, 84

Wilmcote 85

Frith Book Co Titles

www.francisfrith.co.uk

The Frith Book Company publishes over 100 new titles each year. A selection of those currently available are listed below. For latest catalogue please contact Frith Book Co.

Town Books 96 pages, approx 100 photos. County and Themed Books 128 pages, approx 150 photos (unless specified). All titles hardback laminated case and jacket except those indicated pb (paperback)

Amersham, Chesham & Rickmansworth (pb)			Derby (pb)	1-85937-367-4	£9.99
	1-85937-340-2	£9.99	Derbyshire (pb)	1-85937-196-5	£9.99
Ancient Monuments & Stone Circles	1-85937-143-4	£17.99	Devon (pb)	1-85937-297-x	£9.99
Aylesbury (pb)	1-85937-227-9	£9.99	Dorset (pb)	1-85937-269-4	£9.99
Bakewell	1-85937-113-2	£12.99	Dorset Churches	1-85937-172-8	£17.99
Barnstaple (pb)	1-85937-300-3	£9.99	Dorset Coast (pb)	1-85937-299-6	£9.99
Bath (pb)	1-85937419-0	£9.99	Dorset Living Memories	1-85937-210-4	£14.99
Bedford (pb)	1-85937-205-8	£9.99	Down the Severn	1-85937-118-3	£14.99
Berkshire (pb)	1-85937-191-4	£9.99	Down the Thames (pb)	1-85937-278-3	£9.99
Berkshire Churches	1-85937-170-1	£17.99	Down the Trent	1-85937-311-9	£14.99
Blackpool (pb)	1-85937-382-8	£9.99	Dublin (pb)	1-85937-231-7	£9.99
Bognor Regis (pb)	1-85937-431-x	£9.99	East Anglia (pb)	1-85937-265-1	£9.99
Bournemouth	1-85937-067-5	£12.99	East London	1-85937-080-2	£14.99
Bradford (pb)	1-85937-204-x	£9.99	East Sussex	1-85937-130-2	£14.99
Brighton & Hove(pb)	1-85937-192-2	£8.99	Eastbourne	1-85937-061-6	£12.99
Bristol (pb)	1-85937-264-3	£9.99	Edinburgh (pb)	1-85937-193-0	£8.99
British Life A Century Ago (pb)	1-85937-213-9	£9.99	England in the 1880s	1-85937-331-3	£17.99
Buckinghamshire (pb)	1-85937-200-7	£9.99	English Castles (pb)	1-85937-434-4	£9.99
Camberley (pb)	1-85937-222-8	£9.99	English Country Houses	1-85937-161-2	£17.99
Cambridge (pb)	1-85937-422-0	£9.99	Essex (pb)	1-85937-270-8	£9.99
Cambridgeshire (pb)	1-85937-420-4	£9.99	Exeter	1-85937-126-4	£12.99
Canals & Waterways (pb)	1-85937-291-0	£9.99	Exmoor	1-85937-132-9	£14.99
Canterbury Cathedral (pb)	1-85937-179-5	£9.99	Falmouth	1-85937-066-7	£12.99
Cardiff (pb)	1-85937-093-4	£9.99	Folkestone (pb)	1-85937-124-8	£9.99
Carmarthenshire	1-85937-216-3	£14.99	Glasgow (pb)	1-85937-190-6	£9.99
Chelmsford (pb)	1-85937-310-0	£9.99	Gloucestershire	1-85937-102-7	£14.99
Cheltenham (pb)	1-85937-095-0	£9.99	Great Yarmouth (pb)	1-85937-426-3	£9.99
Cheshire (pb)	1-85937-271-6	£9.99	Greater Manchester (pb)	1-85937-266-x	£9.99
Chester	1-85937-090-x	£12.99	Guildford (pb)	1-85937-410-7	£9.99
Chesterfield	1-85937-378-x	£9.99	Hampshire (pb)	1-85937-279-1	£9.99
Chichester (pb)	1-85937-228-7	£9.99	Hampshire Churches (pb)	1-85937-207-4	£9.99
Colchester (pb)	1-85937-188-4	£8.99	Harrogate	1-85937-423-9	£9.99
Cornish Coast	1-85937-163-9	£14.99	Hastings & Bexhill (pb)	1-85937-131-0	£9.99
Cornwall (pb)	1-85937-229-5	£9.99	Heart of Lancashire (pb)	1-85937-197-3	£9.99
Cornwall Living Memories	1-85937-248-1	£14.99	Helston (pb)	1-85937-214-7	£9.99
Cotswolds (pb)	1-85937-230-9	£9.99	Hereford (pb)	1-85937-175-2	£9.99
Cotswolds Living Memories	1-85937-255-4	£14.99	Herefordshire	1-85937-174-4	£14.99
County Durham	1-85937-123-x	£14.99	Hertfordshire (pb)	1-85937-247-3	£9.99
Croydon Living Memories	1-85937-162-0	£9.99	Horsham (pb)	1-85937-432-8	£9.99
Cumbria	1-85937-101-9	£14.99	Humberside	1-85937-215-5	£14.99
Dartmoor	1-85937-145-0	£14.99	Hythe, Romney Marsh & Ashford	1-85937-256-2	£9.99

Available from your local bookshop or from the publisher

Frith Book Co Titles (continued)

Ipswich (pb)	1-85937-424-7	£9.99	St Ives (pb)	1-85937415-8	£9.99
Ireland (pb)	1-85937-181-7	£9.99	Scotland (pb)	1-85937-182-5	£9.99
Isle of Man (pb)	1-85937-268-6	£9.99	Scottish Castles (pb)	1-85937-323-2	£9.99
Isles of Scilly	1-85937-136-1	£14.99	Sevenoaks & Tunbridge	1-85937-057-8	£12.99
Isle of Wight (pb)	1-85937-429-8	£9.99	Sheffield, South Yorks (pb)	1-85937-267-8	£9.99
Isle of Wight Living Memories	1-85937-304-6	£14.99	Shrewsbury (pb)	1-85937-325-9	£9.99
Kent (pb)	1-85937-189-2	£9.99	Shropshire (pb)	1-85937-326-7	£9.99
Kent Living Memories	1-85937-125-6	£14.99	Somerset	1-85937-153-1	£14.99
Lake District (pb)	1-85937-275-9	£9.99	South Devon Coast	1-85937-107-8	£14.99
Lancaster, Morecambe & Heysham (pb)	1-85937-233-3	£9.99	South Devon Living Memories	1-85937-168-x	£14.99
Leeds (pb)	1-85937-202-3	£9.99	South Hams	1-85937-220-1	£14.99
Leicester	1-85937-073-x	£12.99	Southampton (pb)	1-85937-427-1	£9.99
Leicestershire (pb)	1-85937-185-x	£9.99	Southport (pb)	1-85937-425-5	£9.99
Lincolnshire (pb)	1-85937-433-6	£9.99	Staffordshire	1-85937-047-0	£12.99
Liverpool & Merseyside (pb)	1-85937-234-1	£9.99	Stratford upon Avon	1-85937-098-5	£12.99
London (pb)	1-85937-183-3	£9.99	Suffolk (pb)	1-85937-221-x	£9.99
Ludlow (pb)	1-85937-176-0	£9.99	Suffolk Coast	1-85937-259-7	£14.99
Luton (pb)	1-85937-235-x	£9.99	Surrey (pb)	1-85937-240-6	£9.99
Maidstone	1-85937-056-x	£14.99	Sussex (pb)	1-85937-184-1	£9.99
Manchester (pb)	1-85937-198-1	£9.99	Swansea (pb)	1-85937-167-1	£9.99
Middlesex	1-85937-158-2	£14.99	Tees Valley & Cleveland	1-85937-211-2	£14.99
New Forest	1-85937-128-0	£14.99	Thanet (pb)	1-85937-116-7	£9.99
Newark (pb)	1-85937-366-6	£9.99	Tiverton (pb)	1-85937-178-7	£9.99
Newport, Wales (pb)	1-85937-258-9	£9.99	Torbay	1-85937-063-2	£12.99
Newquay (pb)	1-85937-421-2	£9.99	Truro	1-85937-147-7	£12.99
Norfolk (pb)	1-85937-195-7	£9.99	Victorian and Edwardian Cornwall	1-85937-252-x	£14.99
Norfolk Living Memories	1-85937-217-1	£14.99	Victorian & Edwardian Devon	1-85937-253-8	£14.99
Northamptonshire	1-85937-150-7	£14.99	Victorian & Edwardian Kent	1-85937-149-3	£14.99
Northumberland Tyne & Wear (pb)	1-85937-281-3	£9.99	Vic & Ed Maritime Album	1-85937-144-2	£17.99
North Devon Coast	1-85937-146-9	£14.99	Victorian and Edwardian Sussex	1-85937-157-4	£14.99
North Devon Living Memories	1-85937-261-9	£14.99	Victorian & Edwardian Yorkshire	1-85937-154-x	£14.99
North London	1-85937-206-6	£14.99	Victorian Seaside	1-85937-159-0	£17.99
North Wales (pb)	1-85937-298-8	£9.99	Villages of Devon (pb)	1-85937-293-7	£9.99
North Yorkshire (pb)	1-85937-236-8	£9.99	Villages of Kent (pb)	1-85937-294-5	£9.99
Norwich (pb)	1-85937-194-9	£8.99	Villages of Sussex (pb)	1-85937-295-3	£9.99
Nottingham (pb)	1-85937-324-0	£9.99	Warwickshire (pb)	1-85937-203-1	£9.99
Nottinghamshire (pb)	1-85937-187-6	£9.99	Welsh Castles (pb)	1-85937-322-4	£9.99
Oxford (pb)	1-85937-411-5	£9.99	West Midlands (pb)	1-85937-289-9	£9.99
Oxfordshire (pb)	1-85937-430-1	£9.99	West Sussex	1-85937-148-5	£14.99
Peak District (pb)	1-85937-280-5	£9.99	West Yorkshire (pb)	1-85937-201-5	£9.99
Penzance	1-85937-069-1	£12.99	Weymouth (pb)	1-85937-209-0	£9.99
Peterborough (pb)	1-85937-219-8	£9.99	Wiltshire (pb)	1-85937-277-5	£9.99
Piers	1-85937-237-6	£17.99	Wiltshire Churches (pb)	1-85937-171-x	£9.99
Plymouth	1-85937-119-1	£12.99	Wiltshire Living Memories	1-85937-245-7	£14.99
Poole & Sandbanks (pb)	1-85937-251-1	£9.99	Winchester (pb)	1-85937-428-x	£9.99
Preston (pb)	1-85937-212-0	£9.99	Windmills & Watermills	1-85937-242-2	£17.99
Reading (pb)	1-85937-238-4	£9.99	Worcester (pb)	1-85937-165-5	£9.99
Romford (pb)	1-85937-319-4	£9.99	Worcestershire	1-85937-152-3	£14.99
Salisbury (pb)	1-85937-239-2	£9.99	York (pb)	1-85937-199-x	£9.99
Scarborough (pb)	1-85937-379-8	£9.99	Yorkshire (pb)	1-85937-186-8	£9.99
St Albans (pb)	1-85937-341-0	£9.99	Yorkshire Living Memories	1-85937-166-3	£14.99

See Frith books on the internet www.francisfrith.co.uk

FRITH PRODUCTS & SERVICES

Francis Frith would doubtless be pleased to know that the pioneering publishing venture he started in 1860 still continues today. A hundred and forty years later, The Francis Frith Collection continues in the same innovative tradition and is now one of the foremost publishers of vintage photographs in the world. Some of the current activities include:

Interior Decoration

Today Frith's photographs can be seen framed and as giant wall murals in thousands of pubs, restaurants, hotels, banks, retail stores and other public buildings throughout the country. In every case they enhance the unique local atmosphere of the places they depict and provide reminders of gentler days in an increasingly busy and frenetic world.

Product Promotions

Frith products are used by many major companies to promote the sales of their own products or to reinforce their own history and heritage. Frith promotions have been used by Hovis bread, Courage beers, Scots Porage Oats, Colman's mustard, Cadbury's foods, Mellow Birds coffee, Dunhill pipe tobacco, Guinness, and Bulmer's Cider.

Genealogy and Family History

As the interest in family history and roots grows world-wide, more and more people are turning to Frith's photographs of Great Britain for images of the towns, villages and streets where their ancestors lived; and, of course, photographs of the churches and chapels where their ancestors were christened, married and buried are an essential part of every genealogy tree and family album.

Frith Products

All Frith photographs are available Framed or just as Mounted Prints and Posters (size 23 x 16 inches). These may be ordered from the address below. From time to time other products - Address Books, Calendars, Table Mats, etc - are available.

The Internet

Already twenty thousand Frith photographs can be viewed and purchased on the internet through the Frith websites and a myriad of partner sites.

For more detailed information on Frith companies and products, look at these sites:

www.francisfrith.co.uk
www.francisfrith.com
(for North American visitors)

See the complete list of Frith Books at:

www.francisfrith.co.uk

This web site is regularly updated with the latest list of publications from the Frith Book Company. If you wish to buy books relating to another part of the country that your local bookshop does not stock, you may purchase on-line.

For further information, trade, or author enquiries please contact us at the address below:
The Francis Frith Collection, Frith's Barn, Teffont, Salisbury, Wiltshire, England SP3 5QP.
Tel: +44 (0)1722 716 376 Fax: +44 (0)1722 716 881 Email: sales@francisfrith.co.uk

See Frith books on the internet www.francisfrith.co.uk

TO RECEIVE YOUR FREE MOUNTED PRINT

Mounted Print
Overall size 14 x 11 inches

Cut out this Voucher and return it with your remittance for £2.25 to cover postage and handling, to UK addresses. For overseas addresses please include £4.00 post and handling. Choose any photograph included in this book. Your SEPIA print will be A4 in size, and mounted in a cream mount with burgundy rule line, overall size 14 x 11 inches.

Order additional Mounted Prints at HALF PRICE (only £7.49 each*)

If there are further pictures you would like to order, possibly as gifts for friends and family, purchase them at half price (no additional postage and handling required).

Have your Mounted Prints framed*

For an additional £14.95 per print you can have your chosen Mounted Print framed in an elegant polished wood and gilt moulding, overall size 16 x 13 inches (no additional postage and handling required).

---

* IMPORTANT!
These special prices are only available if ordered using the original voucher on this page (no copies permitted) and at the same time as your free Mounted Print, for delivery to the same address

---

Frith Collectors' Guild

From time to time we publish a magazine of news and stories about Frith photographs and further special offers of Frith products. If you would like 12 months FREE membership, please return this form.

Send completed forms to:
The Francis Frith Collection, Frith's Barn, Teffont, Salisbury, Wiltshire SP3 5QP

Voucher for FREE and Reduced Price Frith Prints

Picture no.	Page number	Qty	Mounted @ £7.49	Framed + £14.95	Total Cost
		1	**Free of charge***	£	£
			£7.49	£	£
			£7.49	£	£
			£7.49	£	£
			£7.49	£	£
			£7.49	£	£

Please allow 28 days for delivery	*** Post & handling**	**£2.25**
Book Title	**Total Order Cost**	£

Please do not photocopy this voucher. Only the original is valid, so please cut it out and return it to us.

I enclose a cheque / postal order for £ . . . .
made payable to 'The Francis Frith Collection'
OR please debit my Mastercard / Visa / Switch / Amex card
(credit cards please on all overseas orders)

Number . . . .

Issue No(Switch only) . . . . .Valid from (Amex/Switch) . . . .

Expires . . . . Signature . . . .

Name Mr/Mrs/Ms . . . .

Address . . . .

. . . .

. . . .

Postcode . . . . Daytime Tel No . . . .

Email Address . . . .

VALID TO 31/12/05

The Francis Frith Collectors' Guild

Please enrol me as a member for 12 months free of charge.

Name Mr/Mrs/Ms . . . .

Address . . . .

. . . .

. . . . Postcode . . . .

Would you like to find out more about Francis Frith?

We have recently recruited some entertaining speakers who are happy to visit local groups, clubs and societies to give an illustrated talk documenting Frith's travels and photographs. If you are a member of such a group and are interested in hosting a presentation, we would love to hear from you.

Our speakers bring with them a small selection of our local town and county books, together with sample prints. They are happy to take orders. A small proportion of the order value is donated to the group who have hosted the presentation. The talks are therefore an excellent way of fundraising for small groups and societies.

Can you help us with information about any of the Frith photographs in this book?

We are gradually compiling an historical record for each of the photographs in the Frith archive. It is always fascinating to find out the names of the people shown in the pictures, as well as insights into the shops, buildings and other features depicted.

If you recognize anyone in the photographs in this book, or if you have information not already included in the author's caption, do let us know. We would love to hear from you, and will try to publish it in future books or articles.

Our production team

Frith books are produced by a small dedicated team at offices in the converted Grade II listed 18th-century barn at Teffont near Salisbury, illustrated above. Most have worked with the Frith Collection for many years. All have in common one quality: they have a passion for the Frith Collection. The team is constantly expanding, but currently includes:

Jason Buck, John Buck, Douglas Burns, Ruth Butler, Angie Chick, Heather Crisp, Isobel Hall, Hazel Heaton, Peter Horne, James Kinnear, Tina Leary, Hannah Marsh, Sue Molloy, Kate Rotondetto, Dean Scource, Eliza Sackett, Terence Sackett, Sandra Sanger, Lewis Taylor, Shelley Tolcher, Clive Wathen and Jenny Wathen.